THE
CAMPAIGN
of
1760
In
CANADA

CHEVALIER JOHNSTONE.

[ZHINGOORA BOOKS]

This edition is published by
Zhingoora Books.

The Cover is Designed by Pallav Sethiya.

[Published under the Auspices of the Literary and Historical Society of Quebec.]

The Campaign of 1760 in Canada.

A Sequel

ATTRIBUTED TO CHEVALIER JOHNSTONE.

Hope that heavenly, healing balm, that gift from Providence, blended with persecutions to blunt the sharpness of their sting and hinder the unfortunate from being overwhelmed, and sinking under the load of their afflictions, never dies out—never abandons the distressed. "We don't believe in dangers," says Machiavel, "until they are over our heads; but we entertain hopes of escaping them when at a great distance." Hope does not abandon the pale, dying man: in his agony he still fells life, and in his thoughts he does not detach himself from it. Death strikes, before his heart has realized that he could cease to live. Search in the prisons: hope dwells there with the wretch who next day is to undergo his sentence of death. Every time the bolts rattle, he believes his deliverance entering with the jailer. Whole years of slavery have not been able to wear out this consoling sentiment. These contradictions,—these differences of seeing,—these returns,—this stormy flow and ebb, are so many effects of hope, which plays upon us and never ceases. It is inherent in human nature to hope in adversity for a favorable change of fate, however the appearances may be ill-grounded of an end to its pain and suffering.

The Canadians, without the least apparent reason, still flattered themselves to save their country, and did not lose the hope of retaking Quebec, though without artillery and warlike stores. All minds were occupied during the winter in forming projects of capturing that town, which were entirely chimerical, void of common sense, and nowise practicable. No country ever hatched a greater number—never projects more ridiculous and extravagant; everybody meddled. The contagion spread even to my Lord Bishop and his seminary of priests, who gave their plan, which, like all the others, lacked only common sense and judgment. In short, a universal insanity prevailed at Montreal. Amongst thousands of the productions of these distempered brains, that of surprising Quebec by a forced march in winter and taking it by escalade, was the only one where there was the least chance of success. This project was for some time agitated so seriously, that workmen were employed in making wooden ladders; but having always looked upon it as a wild and extravagant fancy of priests and old women, I constantly argued against it whenever they spoke of it, and it was continually the topic of conversation.

The Upper Town of Quebec lies upon the top of a rock, about two hundred feet high, almost perpendicular in some parts of it, and everywhere extremely steep and inaccessible, excepting towards the *Hauteurs d'Abraham*, which is a continuation of the same hill, that begins at Quebec and ends at Cap Rouge, diminishing gradually in height in the space of these three leagues. The Lower Town is a narrow piece of ground, from a hundred to four or five paces[A] broad, between the foot of the rock and the St. Lawrence.

There is a street which goes up to the Upper Town without a continuation of houses; it is impossible to climb up the rock from the Lower Town, as I was employed three weeks upon it with miners an other workmen, to render all the footpaths impracticable; we finished only a few days before the arrival of the English fleet (in 1759). A town built upon a vast extent of ground, which would require an army to defend it, such as Ghent in Flanders, and which might be approached on all sides at the same time, in order to divide the troops of the garrison equally over all the town, may be surprised and taken by escalade, and in our desperate situation might have been attempted by risking all for all. A surprise in a dark night must naturally spread universal terror, disorder and panic amongst those who are taken unawares, and must soon be communicated through all the quarters of the town. The soldiers are so much the more terrified that they know not where they are most in danger; not like during a siege, where the place for the assault is marked by the breach. Their heads turn, and, deprived of judgment, coolness and reflection, they think rather of escaping the slaughter that ensues when a town is being captured in this manner, than of defending the ramparts. But Quebec being accessible only on that side of it which faces the heights of Abraham, and having nothing to fear elsewhere, the moment an alarm is sounded, all the force of the garrison must naturally be there. Thus the English having seven thousand men in the town—almost as many as our army proposed for the escalade to invest all that part of the town open to attack—it is likely that we should have lost the half of our army in the attempt, and at last, after a horrible slaughter of men, have been obliged to return ignominiously from whence we came. Besides, supposing that we had even taken the Lower Town by escalade, we would not have been further advanced. The English, in half an hour afterwards, by burning it, by throwing down from the Upper Town upon the roofs of the houses fire pots, shells and other combustible matter, could have soon chased us out of it, or buried us under its ruins. This project, after having furnished for a long time matter for the daily conversations of Montrealers, was at last considered by M. de Levis, and classed as it deserved, amongst the vagaries of bedlam; he substituting a scheme in its place which was reasonable, well combined, doing honor to his ability and talent.

[A] The four or five paces of 1760 have now attained seven or eight acres.— (L)

M. de Levis, in giving an account to the Court of the loss of all our artillery and stores at Quebec, gave likewise all possible assurances that he would re-take the town in the spring and save the colony, provided they would send to him from Europe a ship loaded with field-pieces and ammunition, to set sail from Europe in the month of February, in order to be in the St. Lawrence river before the arrival of the English, and near Quebec in the month of April. He collected our army as soon as the season permitted; got together about twelve pieces of old cannon, which had been laid aside for many years, and with a small quantity of gunpowder and very few bullets, he set out from Montreal with his army towards the beginning of April, the snow being as yet upon the ground; and he conducted his march so well that the army arrived at Cap Rouge, three leagues from Quebec, without the enemy having any information of their having left Montreal. He did not flatter himself to be able to take Quebec with such a despicable train of artillery, and his design was only to invest the town; to open the trenches before it; to advance his approaches, and be in a position, the moment the ships he had asked from the Court should arrive, to land the cannon, placing them instantly upon the batteries ready to receive them, and without loss of time to batter the town immediately.

Fortune favored him to the height of his wishes, and if the ships had arrived with the artillery he expected from France, that town could scarce have held out for four and twenty hours, by which means he would have had the glory of preserving to his country the colony of Canada, then reduced to its last gasp.

The English got the news of our army's being at Cap Rouge by a most singular accident, which greatly manifests the predominant power of Fortune in military operations, and shows that the greatest general cannot guarantee success or put himself out of the reach of those events which human understanding cannot foresee, whereby the best combined and well-formed schemes are frustrated in their execution. In all appearance we would have taken Quebec by surprise had it not been for one of Fortune's caprices, that have often as much share in the events of war as the genius and talents of the greatest generals.

The Athenians were not in the wrong to paint Timotheus asleep, whilst Fortune, in another part of the picture, was spreading nets over towns to take them for him.

An artillery boat having been overturned and sunk by the sheets of ice, which the current of the St. Lawrence brought down with great force, an artilleryman saved himself on a piece of ice that floated down the river with him upon it, without a possibility of his getting to land, when he was opposite to the city.

The English, so soon as they perceived that poor distressed man—moved with humanity and compassion—sent out boats, who with difficulty saved him (the river being covered with fields of ice), and brought him to town with scarce any sign of life. Having restored him with cordials, the moment he began to breathe and recover his senses, they asked him from whence he came, and who he was? he answered, innocently, that he was a French cannonier from M. de Levis' army at Cap Rouge. At first they imagined he raved, and that his sufferings upon the river had turned his head; but, after examining him more particularly and his answers being always the same, they were soon convinced of the truth of his assertions, and were not a little confounded to have the French army at three leagues from Quebec, without possessing the smallest information of the fact. All their care proved ineffectual for the preservation of life; he expired the moment he had revealed this important secret. What a remarkable and visible instance of fortune fighting for the English—equal at least to the cloud of rain that saved General Wolfe's army the year preceding at his attack of 31st of July, at Montmorenci. Had it not been for this most unaccountable accident, to all appearance M. de Levis would have captured all the English advanced posts, which were said to amount to fifteen hundred men, who retired to the town immediately after setting fire to the magazine of powder in the church of St. Foy, which ammunition they had not the time to carry with them.

Nor would it have been surprising if M. de Levis, at the gates of Quebec with his army, without being discovered, had taken it by surprise. It is certain that luck has more or less share in all the events of life, and this is more particularly visible in the operations of war. Hazards may be constantly in the favor of a general blindly protected by that goddess, against an adversary with far superior talents. Everybody must acknowledge Prince Eugene's superiority of genius, when compared with the Duke of Marlborough; but Marlborough was always as fortunate in having continually unforeseen accidents in his favor, as Prince Eugene was unlucky to have them against him to thwart and cross the execution of the best-combined projects, which extorted admiration, and seemed to have only need of Fortune's standing neuter to be successful. The fate of an army,—can it depend upon the personal good fortune of the General who commands it? Cardinal Mazarin seemed to be of this opinion, since he never failed to ask those who recommended persons to him to head expeditions, "is he lucky?"—*est-il heureux*? Can it be surmised that fortune acts with her favorite sons at the head of armies, as she does at gambling tables? However it may be, a great General will always watch vigilantly the chapter of accidents—seize rapidly that which is favorable to him, and, by his prudence, foresight and circumspection, will ward off and correct what is contrary to his interests. The smallest things are not unworthy of his attention; they often produce the greatest events, and the neglecting what at first view might appear trivial, has often overturned the best-calculated schemes. The most trifling of our actions becomes often a first cause which produces an endless chain of effects—linked to each other—of the greatest importance. The boat sunk by the ice, at Cap Rouge, was a first cause. The cannonier, by this accident, was upon a sheet of ice in the middle of the St. Lawrence, opposite to Quebec; this inspired with pity the English to save his life. This humane action of the English in saving the unhappy cannonier, saved Quebec from being taken by surprise, which probably would have been the case without his information, that M. de Levis' army was at Cap Rouge. If taken by M. de Levis, it would have deterred the English from any further attempt upon Canada, and peace would have soon ensued. But by the cannonier's declaration, it was not taken, and consequently the war was prolonged.

Quebec in possession of the English rendered the conquest of Canada inevitable and sure. The possession of that vast country of Canada, after so much blood, and such immense expenses it had cost the English in these different expeditions, excited too much the cupidity of the English to consent to a peace upon reasonable conditions, and induced them to extend their conquest to other French colonies.

The possession of so many French and Spanish colonies by the English brought about the shameful peace that France and Spain were obliged to receive at the hands of the English, upon the hardest terms, as laws of the conqueror.

The boat upset and sunk at Cap Rouge was the primary cause and the first link of the chain which had the greatest influence over all the affairs of Europe. If M. de Levis had saved the cannonier at Cap Rouge, what a multitude of events would have been nipped in the bud! Perhaps even Great Britain would have been forced to receive the peace from France instead of granting it on her own conditions.

There is scarcely any human action that is not the beginning of a chain of results.

The French army took possession of the village of St. Foye the moment the English went out of it, retiring to Quebec, and passed there the night between the 27th and 28th of April. Next morning M. de Levis being informed that the English army was come out of the town, and that they were drawn up in battle upon the same ground that the French army had occupied the year before at the battle of the 13th September, he drew out his men and advanced in order of battle to meet the English army. Though fully persuaded that the English general would not risk a battle out of his town, where he had a great deal to lose in being beat, and could gain little by a victory, he was fully persuaded that he would return at the approach of the French army.

General Murray, who does the greatest honor to his country by his great knowledge of the art of war, good sense and ability, had come out of the town in order to cover that place with a retrenchment, which was very evident from the prodigious quantity of working tools that were taken by the French; and the vast rapidity with which the French army advanced in all appearance, deprived him of the possibility of getting back into Quebec without leaving a part of them to be cut to pieces by the Canadians.

The English army had the advantage of position. They were drawn up in battle upon rising ground, their front armed with twenty-two brass field-pieces—the Palace battery which De Ramsay refused to send to M. de Montcalm. The engagement began by the attack of a house (Dumont's) between the right wing of the English army and the French left wing, which was alternately attacked and defended by the Scotch Highlanders and the French Grenadiers, each of them taking it and losing it by turns. Worthy antagonists!—the Grenadiers, with their bayonets in their hands, forced the Highlanders to get out of it by the windows; and the Highlanders getting into it again by the door, immediately obliged the Grenadiers to evacuate it by the same road, with their daggers. Both of them lost and retook the house[B] several times, and the contest would have continued whilst there remained a Highlander and a Grenadier, if both generals had not made them retire, leaving the house neuter ground. The Grenadiers were reduced to fourteen men—a company at most. No doubt the Highlanders lost in proportion. The left of the French army, which was in hollow ground, about forty paces from the English, was crushed to pieces by the fire of their artillery loaded with grape-shot. M. de Levis, perceiving their bad position, sent M. de La Pause, Adjutant of the Guienne Regiment, with orders for the army to retire some steps behind them, in order to occupy an eminence parallel to the rising ground occupied by the English; but whether this officer did not comprehend M. de Levis' intentions, or whether he delivered ill the orders to the different regiments, by his stupidity the battle was very near being lost irremediably. He ran along the line, ordering each regiment to the right about, and to retire, without any further explanation of M. de Levis' orders. Some of the left of the French army being so near as twenty paces to the enemy, the best disciplined troops in that case can scarce be expected to be able to retire without the greatest disorder and confusion, or without exposing themselves evidently to be defeated and slaughtered. Upon this movement, the English, believing them in flight, quitted their advantage of the rising ground in order to pursue them, complete their disorder, and break them entirely. M. Dalquier, who commanded the Bearn Regiment, with the troops of the colony upon the left of the French army, a bold, intrepid old officer, turned about to his soldiers when La Pause gave him M. de Levis' order to retire, and told them, "It is not time now, my boys, to retire when at twenty paces from the enemy; with your bayonets upon your muskets, let us throw ourselves headlong amongst them—that is better." In an instant they fell upon the English impetuously—with thrusts of bayonets hand to hand, got possession, like lightning, of their guns; and a ball which went through Dalquier's body, which was already quite covered with scars of old wounds, did not hinder him from continuing giving his orders. Poularies, who was on the right flank of the army, with his regiment of Royal Roussillon, and some of the Canadian militia, seeing Dalquier stand firm, and all the troops of the centre having retired in disorder, leaving a space between the two wings, he caused his regiment with the Canadians to wheel to the left, in order to fall upon the left flank of the English army, the French army extending further to their right beyond the English left wing. The enemy no sooner perceived Poularies' movement, than they immediately fled with precipitation and confusion, and were so panic-stricken that not an English soldier could be rallied by their officers, several of whom were taken prisoners. The French troops who had retired advanced immediately, and all the French army pursued so hotly the English, that if the cry had not been raised to halt, it is very doubtful if they would not have got into Quebec pell-mell with the fugitives, being near the town-gates when this cry began. Thus Quebec would have been retaken in a most singular manner,[C] unforeseen and unpremeditated. I know nothing worse than ill-disciplined troops; certainly a brave militia, with its simple, ancient way of fighting, even not drilled, is preferable to a force having a crude notion of discipline—a science entirely neglected in Canada amongst French regular troops; so that the French regiments there might be looked upon as differing very little from the Canadian militia. The method of managing militia and well-disciplined regular troops appears to be quite as different as they differ in nature. A cool, phlegmatic, undaunted bravery is the fruit of an excellent discipline, rendering the soldiers capable, when repulsed, to return several times to the assault, and rally of their own accord. But the strength and merit of the militia resembles a hot, ardent, raging fire, that must be suffered to blaze until it dies out of itself: it is a flash, an explosion, that often works prodigies, and which, when stifled, there is no possibility of preventing the immediate disorder that must ensue, nor any means of bringing it back a second time to face the enemy.

Note.—The preceding winter had been employed in skirmishing around Quebec.— (J.M.L.)

[B] Dumont's Mill.

[C] "On the night of the eighteenth of March, two hundred light infantry were detached from the Garrison of Quebec, with three days' provisions, and a company of Grenadiers, marched the next day to Lorette Church, being the place of rendezvous. The whole proceeded to Calvaire, accompanied by a French deserter in a British uniform. In this route they surprised an advanced post of the French, and made the party prisoners, consisting of a corporal and nine privates; having secured these, they pushed forward with the greatest speed, fearing that a straggling peasant, whom they met, should mar their further views by alarming the country. The light infantry having reached the wished for object, which was a strong camp or entrenchment of logs and timber, with a house detached at a small distance from it, they carried the dwelling house with their accustomed bravery, killed four and took the rest, being twenty in number, some of whom were wounded. The main body of the French by this time had manned their works, which were breast high, and environed with an abattis of wood, to the distance of about three hundred yards, whence they fired a few random shots and shouted as usual. Capt. McDonald, who commanded this detachment, seeing the French advantageously situated, and perceiving their officers very active in encouraging their men, expected a warm dispute, and therefore made a disposition to attack them in form. As soon, however, as the light infantry advanced to the charge, the French threw down their arms and took to flight, when near eighty of them were made prisoners. In the attack the English had only six wounded; but the French lost five killed and thirteen wounded. Capt. McDonald destroyed the post, three corn-mills, granaries, and other houses contiguous thereto. The French prisoners were brought to Quebec, except the wounded, who were left in charge of the peasants, with directions to conduct them to Jacques Cartier. Near one hundred soldiers of the English detachment were frost-bitten, and were brought back to the garrison on sleighs. Capt. Herbin, the commanding officer, escaped; but his watch, hat, and feather, 'fille de joie,' with a cask of wine and case of liqueurs, were taken.

"The Governor of Quebec (General Murray) sent the Town Major to the Mother Abbess of the Convent of Hotel Dieu, to acquaint her with the reasons that induced him to destroy their mills and tenements at Calvaire: namely, on account of her having transmitted intelligence to the French, of the last detachment's being ordered to be in readiness to march out; for having actually carried on a correspondence with the French army in the whole course of the winter, whereby they were informed of all movements, proceedings, and every other occurrence that happened within the walls: the Governor also signified to her, that if either she or her sisters should presume to correspond in future with the French, either directly or indirectly, or in any respect act contrary to good faith and the duty they owed to the King of Great Britain, they should, without further ceremony, be banished from Quebec, and their convent be converted into a barrack for the troops. As Madame de St. Claude, who was sister to M. de Ramsay, and Superior of the General Hospital, had always been inimical to the English in propagating falsehoods, and in encouraging the

Canadians to resist, General Murray sent the Brigade-Major to signify to this lady that she should desist from such conduct; and that as she appeared to take a great interest in the affairs of this world, and seemed tired of her seclusion, he would enlist her as a Grenadier, which from her stature (full six feet) she was qualified to be, and that he would promote her the first opportunity that presented itself."—(Smith.)

The French had about two thousand killed and wounded in this battle of the 27th (? 28th) of April, of which number there was an hundred and ten officers of the regular troops, besides a great many officers of the Canadian militia: so they might say with Pyrrhus, the day of his victory over the Romans—"Again such another victory, and I would be undone!"

M. de Levis opened the trenches the same night before Quebec, and they were carried on with such activity that his batteries were soon ready to receive the guns necessary to make a breach.

But the most considerable of his bad pieces was a twelve pounder, which he mounted upon batteries, firing at times with the greatest economy, as he had but a small store of gunpowder. There needed only the arrival of a ship from France with artillery and ammunition to crown M. de Levis with glory. The English in Quebec confessed that the first flag that would appear in the St. Lawrence would decide the question, if Canada should remain in possession of the English or return to the French.

No ships arrived from France with artillery. The fate of Canada was at last settled by the appearance of three English men-of-war, on the 7th of May. They ascended immediately the St. Lawrence without stopping at Quebec. They attacked the small French frigates—at the Ance du Foulon, about a mile above the town—which had passed the winter in Canada; took some of them, burned others, and, in short, destroyed in an instant all the French marine. This unlooked-for arrival, instead of the vessel which M. de Levis expected from France, so astonished and terrified the French army, that they immediately raised the siege—and that without any necessity for it. They again left as a present for the English their tents and their baggage, as they had done previously on retiring from Beauport, after the battle of the 13th September. Such was their consternation that, as if struck by a thunderbolt, they fled with the utmost precipitation, as if the English were pursuing them after the loss of a battle. De Vauquelin alone distinguished himself by a truly heroic bravery. He commanded one of the small French frigates of about sixteen guns, and fought like a lion against an English man-of-war of forty guns, until he had no powder nor shot. He then sent all his crew ashore to M. de Levis, judging that they might be of use to him, and remained on board with the wounded, his colors always flying.

The English, after firing some time at his vessel, and receiving no answer, approached in their boats and asked him why he did not fire, or lower his flag? De Vauquelin answered them fiercely that, had he had any more powder he would not have been silent so long; that if they had a mind to take him, they might cut down his flag themselves, as hitherto his custom was not to strike his colors, but to make others—his country's enemies—do so. The English then went on board of his ship, and took him prisoner, with his wounded men, and in consideration of his determination—they having cut down his flag—treated him with the regard which bravery can claim at the hands of a generous enemy. De Vauquelin had already made himself known to the English by his undaunted courage at the siege of Louisburg. His intrepidity so delighted the English Admiral, that he begged him to tell him freely how he could serve him. He answered the Admiral, "that what he wished for of all things was to have his liberty and permission to return to France." The Admiral had so great a consideration for him, that he caused a vessel to be immediately fitted out to carry him to Europe, ordering the English captain to obey De Vauquelin and land him in any French port he might ask for, leaving him at the same time to choose what French passengers would accompany him. This noble and generous behaviour of the English did honor to their nation, by rendering justice to, and discerning the merit of, an enemy, far beyond what De Vauquelin met with from Berryer, the Secretary of the Navy, on his arrival in France.

The unhappy situation of the colony was now past remedy, and may be compared to a man in the agonies of death, to whom the physician continues to administer cordials, not from hopes of his recovery, but to allay and soften the violence of his sufferings. All that could now be expected was to obtain an honorable capitulation, favorable to its inhabitants, the colony being at its last gasp.

M. de Levis left two thousand men at Jacques Cartier, with orders to retire slowly according as the English advanced from Quebec, and to avoid an engagement with them, without losing sight of them. This retarded their march, and put off the evil hour as long as possible. He went with the rest of his army to Montreal. As there was no provision in that town to be able to keep his army assembled, he was obliged to disperse them, sending them back to their winter quarters, where each inhabitant was obliged to board a soldier at a very low rate, which was paid by the munitionary general.

M. de Bougainville was sent in the spring to command at Isle aux Noix, with eleven hundred men, of which number were the Regiment of Guienne and Berry. This island is situated in the River Chambly (Richelieu), about eight leagues in a straight line from Montreal, and two miles distant from Lake Champlain.

M. Bourlamarque, an officer of great knowledge in all the branches of his profession, decided upon that position for his retreat the year before, when he evacuated Ticonderoga, having been forced to abandon to the English that lake. He fortified this island as well as was possible in a sandy ground, in order to serve as a frontier on that side of Canada, and hinder the English from coming down by the River Richelieu into the River St. Lawrence, by which means in a very short time they might have been in possession of Montreal and Three Rivers,—a much easier way than by Lake Ontario, which is much longer and full of chicares (?) by the rapids in the St. Lawrence, and prolong their operations;—a very great advantage in a country where there are violent frosts during seven months of the year. This island is about twelve hundred fathoms long, and from a hundred to two hundred broad. The entrenchments traced and conducted by M. Bourlamarque are regular, and a proof of his superior knowledge in fortifications. He barred the two branches of the river which formed the island with staccados, or chains of big trees, linked to one another at their ends by strong rings and circles of iron. This prevented the English boats from Lake Champlain to pass the island in the night, to reach Montreal. But for the staccados the island must have been taken by them before they could proceed any further.

Some Iroquois, of the Five Nations, informed M. de Vaudreuil at Montreal, that General Amherst was marching to invade Canada with a very considerable army by the rapids and Lake Ontario, whilst General Murray had orders to come up the river with his army from Quebec, and join Gen. Amherst at Montreal. But they had no knowledge of a third body of troops, about four thousand men, that came by Lake Champlain, in the month of July, five weeks before the arrival of the other two armies at Montreal, and besieged Isle aux Noix with a very considerable train of artillery, cannon, mortars, &c., in profusion.

They erected five batteries of guns on the south side of the river, with a bomb battery, which rendered our trenches useless, as they had a sight of us everywhere, back, face and sideways, and so near us that at the south staccado they killed several of our soldiers by their musket shots.

The sandy ground protected us from the effect of their shells, which they threw upon us in great numbers, with a continual fire from their gun batteries.

After sixteen days' siege with a most violent cannonade, without a moment's interruption, M. Nogaire, an officer in the Regiment of Royal Roussillon, came to us from Montreal, having crossed directly through the woods, with some Indians for his guides, with two letters from De Bougainville, one of which was from him to Vaudreuil, and the other from M. de Levis. It was a very critical conjuncture, having only two days' provision for the garrison, which had subsisted until the arrival of the English troops by means of fishing-nets, that river abounding with the most delicious fish, with seven or eight oxen, which had been kept as a reserve and killed by the enemy's cannon. M. de Vaudreuil's letter contained a permission to M. de Bougainville to capitulate or retire from the island if it was possible. M. de Levis' letter was a positive order to defend that post to the last extremity. De Bougainville, notwithstanding his genius, good sense and learning, with personal courage, and who lacked only taste for the study of the art of war to distinguish himself, was nevertheless put to a nonplus how to act from the contradictory orders he received. In this dilemma he shewed me the letters, asking at the same time my advice; and my answer was:—"That in two days famine must oblige us to surrender to the enemy at discretion. That the reinforcements of a thousand men at Montreal might be of the greatest importance, and help to make a good countenance when the English army had advanced in the neighborhood of it. That it was M. de Vaudreuil who commanded-in-chief in Canada, and not M. de Lévis; and that there was yet a possibility of retiring with the garrison towards the north side of the island, where the swampy ground upon the border of the river had hindered the English from establishing a post." De Bougainville immediately decided for a retreat, which was executed and combined with equal justness; and the success answered exactly to the prudence, wisdom and good conduct that De Bougainville exhibited in preparing for it. It was then about ten in the morning when Nogaire arrived with the Indians, who—not accustomed to such a terrible fire as was at that moment poured forth by the English batteries, very different from their way of fighting behind trees—were not at all at ease, and furiously impatient to get out of the island. The hour of retreat was settled for ten that night.

The north shore of Isle aux Noix, on the opposite side of the river, was marshy to the distance of three hundred paces from the river, covered with small trees where there was a rising ground, and there was no English post nearer to it than at the Prairie de Boileau, distant half a mile down the river, so that the locality where the river was fordable was a little below the north staccados. De Bougainville adopted every prudent measure imaginable to achieve success. He ordered all the boats to be mended and put in condition to be used at a moment's warning. He also ordained that the boats, bark canoes, and punts hewn out of a large tree, be removed a certain distance from the river side, lest some soldier should desert and apprise the English of his design, such as had happened from the posts near Quebec. He commanded that all the garrison should be in order of battle at ten at night, all observing a profound silence, without the least clashing of arms or other noise, and be in readiness to march. He ordered M. le Borgne, an officer in the colonial troops, to remain on the island with a detachment of forty men, to keep up a smart fire from our battery, which consisted of seven or eight pieces of cannon, during the time we were employed in passing the river, in order to hinder the English from hearing us in our operations, and to continue firing whilst ammunition lasted, and to conceal our retreat as long as it was possible to do so.

We began to cross the river in two lighters, with some small boats, about ten at night. They plied continually to and fro until midnight, when all had crossed the river without the enemy perceiving or even suspecting our operation, although so near to us were their posts on their left that we heard distinctly their voices. All was executed without the least noise, disorder, or confusion—a rare occurrence on such an occasion. Le Borgne acted well, and at the same time economized his ammunition so well that he had wherewith to fire upon the English at intervals until one in the morning. Imagining us then to be near Montreal, he hoisted the white flag to capitulate, and the English, not having the smallest notion of our retreat, granted him immediately very honorable terms. We had eighty men killed or wounded during the siege—a very inconsiderable loss for a cannonade of sixteen days' duration, from five batteries, besides a bomb battery, without an instant's intermission. Had it been a stony instead of a sandy ground, we must have lost above one-half of the garrison, and could not have resisted so long.

So soon as everyone had passed the river, we set out for Montreal, crossing through the woods, which, in a straight line, is only eight leagues from Isle aux Noix, always half running one after the other, after having marched in this manner, from midnight until twelve at noon, over fens, swamps, mosses, and sinking often up to the waist in marshy ground, without reposing or halting one minute. Instead of being near Montreal, as we imagined, we were thunderstruck on finding ourselves, by the fault of our guides, to be only at the distance of half a league from Isle aux Noix: our guide, not knowing the road through the woods, had caused us to turn round continually for twelve hours without advancing!

We were so near an English post at the Prairie de Boileau, that a grenadier of the Regiment de Berry, seeing his commander, Cormier, sink down with fatigue, and not in a condition to go any further, carried off a horse from them which was upon the borders of the wood, and mounted his commander on it; otherwise he would have been left aside and taken prisoner by the English, or scalped by the Indians.

Having lost all hopes of going to Montreal through the woods, we took the road to Fort St. Jean, on the River Chambly, four leagues lower than Isle aux Noix, and five leagues by land to Montreal. My strength was so entirely spent, that it was with great difficulty I could draw one leg after the other. Nevertheless the fear of falling into the hands of the Indians, the idea of the horrible cruelties which they practice on their prisoners, which shock human nature, prevented me from sinking down with pain, and gave me strength to push on.

Arrived at a settlement at four in the afternoon, about a league and a half from St. John's Fort, where De Bougainville caused his detachment to halt and repose themselves for the first time since midnight, that they left Isle aux Noix. I perceived there a boat going off to St. Jean, and I had only strength enough remaining to throw myself into it. We lost in this march about eighty men: those who could not hold out were left behind, victims to the Indians. Arriving at St. John's Fort, the first person I saw there was Poularies, on the river side, who told me they had news of our retreat, and that he was sent with his regiment to sustain us in case we had been pursued by the English.

We were now shut up in the island of Montreal on all sides. The English were masters of the River Chambly by the possession of Isle aux Noix. General Amherst approached with his army from Lake Ontario; and General Murray was in march, coming up from Quebec, with six thousand men that had passed through the winter there, and with some men-of-war, one of which of about forty guns, on its arrival in sight of the town of Montreal, greatly astonished, and excited the admiration of, the inhabitants, who, from the ignorance and negligence of those persons charged with the sounding of the St. Lawrence, had never seen vessels arrive there of above sixty or seventy tons.

General Murray conducted himself as an officer of great understanding, knowledge and capacity, and left nothing to do for General Amherst; he employed five weeks in coming from Quebec to Montreal, which is only sixty leagues, and did us during his march more harm by his policy than by his army. He stopped often in the villages; spoke kindly to the inhabitants he found at home in their houses—whom hunger and famine had obliged to fly from our army at Montreal; gave provisions to those unhappy creatures perishing for want of subsistence. He burned, in some cases, the houses of those who were absent from home and in the French army at Montreal, publishing everywhere an amnesty and good treatment to all Canadians who would return to their habitations and live there peaceably. In short—flattering some and frightening others—he succeeded so well, that at last there was no more possibility of keeping them at Montreal. It is true we had now only need of them to make a good countenance. The three English armies amounting to above twenty thousand men, it was impossible to make any further resistance.

Amherst's army appeared in sight from the town of Montreal, towards the gate of Lachine, on the 7th of September, about three in the afternoon. General Murray with his army, from Quebec, appeared two hours after at the opposite side of the town: thus a dark crisis was at hand for the fate of Canada. Montreal was nowise susceptible of defence. It was surrounded with stone walls, built in the beginning of that colony, merely to preserve the inhabitants from the incursions of the Indians, few imagining at that time it would become the theatre of a regular war, and that one day they would see formidable armies of regular, well-disciplined troops before its walls.

We were, however, all pent up in that miserable, bad place—without provisions, a thousand times worse off than an advantageous position in open fields—whose pitiful walls could not resist two hours' cannonade without being level with the ground, and where we would have been forced to surrender at discretion, if the English had insisted upon it.

The night between the 7th and 8th September was passed in negotiating for the articles of capitulation. But in the morning all the difficulties were removed, and General Amherst granted conditions infinitely more favourable than could be expected in our circumstances.

Thus the Canadians, as brave as they are docile, and easy to be governed, became subjects of Great Britain; and if they can think themselves happy under that Government, by remembering their past vexations, they will do so.

M. (Col.) Poularies and M. (Col.) Dalquier, who were generally distinguished in the French army by their high sense of honor, probity, and their bravery, experience and knowledge in the art of war, were both of them, on their arrival in France, broken as commanders of a battalion—a grade which was abolished in the French service, in order to make the Major, as in the British service, command the regiment in absence of the Colonel and Lieutenant-Colonel. Belcomb, Poularies' Adjt. of Royal Roussillon, and Montgnary, Captain in the Regiment of Bearn which Dalquier commanded— (two very handsome men, capable to attract the attention of the ladies of any court in Europe)—were made Colonels of Foot, without possessing any remarkable military talent or capacity.

Fortune manifested most cruelly her almighty power in the military state, where justice, punishments and rewards alone ought to be the base of it. Men conduct themselves from the view either of honor or interest; and there can be no emulation in a service where mediocrity of talents, intrigues, favor, and credit, override merit.

Greatness of soul, joined to superiority of talent, ignores the art of cringing; it is even impossible that merit can lead to fortune in a corrupted and venal country: on the contrary, it becomes a cause of exclusion. Virtue elevates the soul, and can neither fawn nor buy credit, nor flatter vice and incapacity. "If such is the military constitution of a State," says M. Gaubert, in his Treatise of Tactics, "of which the Sovereign (the King of Prussia) is one of the greatest men of the age, who instructs and commands his armies, and whose armies form all the pomp of the court, what ought it to be in those States where the Sovereign is not at all a military man; where he does not see his troops; where he seems to disdain or be ignorant of all that regards them; where the Court, who always obey the impression of the Sovereign, is consequently not military; where almost all the great rewards are obtained by surprise, by intrigue; where the greater portion of favors are hereditary; where merit languishes for want of support; where favor can advance without talent; where to make a fortune no more implies acquiring a reputation, but merely to heap up riches; where men may be, at one and the same time, covered with orders and infamy—with grades and ignorance, serve ill the State, and occupy the best places; be smeared with the censure of the public, and enjoy the Sovereign's good graces? If, whilst all other sciences are becoming perfected, that of war remains in its infancy, it is the fault of the Governments, who do not attach to it sufficient importance; who do not make it an object of public education; who fail to direct men of genius to that profession; who suffer them to find more glory and advantages in sciences trifling or less useful; who render the profession of arms an ungrateful employment, where talents are outstripped by intrigue, and the prizes distributed by Fortune."

General Amherst, according to his statement in his letter to Mr. Pitt, then Secretary of State, lost in coming down the rapids—without meeting there any opposition from the French or Indians—by drowning, eighty-four men. Twenty more of the regiments' boats were dashed to pieces. Seven boats of the artillery, loaded with arms and ammunition, and one of his galleys, were also lost.

If 900 Indians had been there, as they should have been, scattered in the woods upon the borders of the river, with 1,200 Canadians, which they had solicited earnestly from M. de Vaudreuil, to defend those difficult passes of the Rapids, but which this officer obstinately refused, what would have become of General Amherst? How could he have got out of the scrape? As it happened to Braddock, Amherst and his army must have perished there; his expedition would have been fruitless, and Canada would have been yet saved to France: but heaven willed it otherwise. How long the English may preserve this conquest depends on their own wise and prudent conduct.

THE END.

[The original of this manuscript is deposited in the French war archives, in Paris: a copy was, with the permission of the French Government, taken by P.L. Morin, Esq., Draughtsman to the Crown Lands Department of Canada, about 1855, and deposited in the Library of the Legislative Assembly of Canada. The Literary and Historical Society of Quebec, through the kindness of Mr. Todd, the Librarian, was permitted to have communication thereof. This document is supposed to have been written some years after the return to France from Canada of the writer, the Chevalier Johnstone, a Scotch Jacobite, who had fled to France after the defeat at Culloden, and had obtained from the French monarch, with several other Scotchmen, commissions in the French armies. In 1748, says *Francisque Michel*,[D] he sailed from Rochefort as an Ensign with troops going to Cape Breton: he continued to serve in America until he returned to France, in December, 1760, having acted during the campaign of 1759, in Canada, as aide-de-camp to Chevalier de Levis. On de Levis being ordered to Montreal, Johnstone was detached and retained by General Montcalm on his staff, on account of his thorough knowledge of the environs of Quebec, and particularly of Beauport, where the principal works of defence stood, and where the whole army, some 11,000 men, were entrenched, leaving in Quebec merely a garrison of 1,500. The journal is written in English, and is not remarkable for orthography or purity of diction: either

Johnstone had forgotten, or had never thoroughly known, the language.]

[D] *Les Ecossais en France*, vol. ii, p. 449.

The End

www.ingramcontent.com/pod-product-compliance
Lightning Source LLC
Chambersburg PA
CBHW060020300526
45794CB00003B/1225